Art and
Civilization

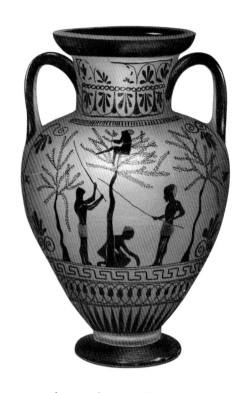

Other titles in the series
Art and Civilization:

Ancient Greece

Matilde Bardi

Illustrations by Paola Ravaglia, Alessandro Cantucci,
Fabiano Fabbrucci, Andrea Morandi, Matteo Chesi

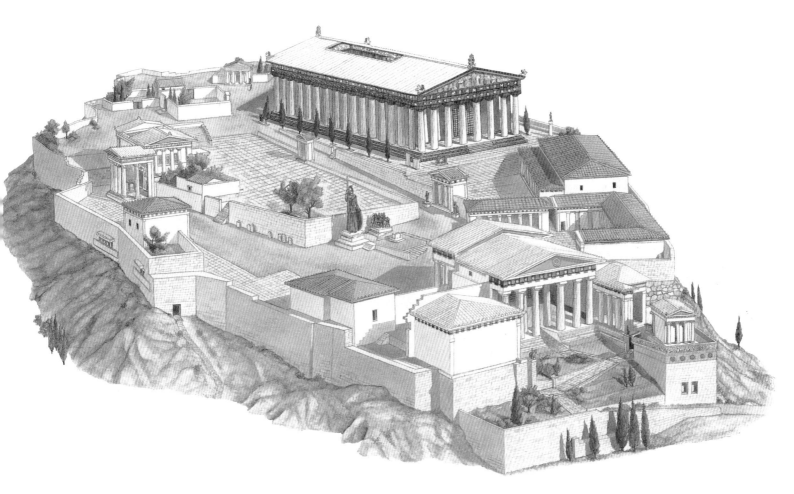

PETER BEDRICK BOOKS

NEW YORK

Published in the United States in 2000
by PETER BEDRICK BOOKS
A division of NTC/Contemporary Publishing Group, Inc.
4255 West Touhy Avenue, Lincolnwood (Chicago), Illinois
60646-1975 U.S.A.
Library of Congress Cataloging-in-Publication CIP data
is available from the United States Library of Congress

Ancient Greece was created and produced by
McRae Books Srl, via de' Rustici, 5 – Florence (Italy)
e-mail: mcrae@tin.it

Text: Matilde Bardi
Main illustrations: Paola Ravaglia, Studio Stalio (Alessandro Cantucci,
Fabiano Fabbrucci, Andrea Morandi), Matteo Chesi
Picture research: Erika Barrow
Graphic Design Marco Nardi, Anne McRae
Editing: Anne McRae
Layout and cutouts: Ornella Fassio, Adriano Nardi
Color separations Fotolito Toscana, Florence and Litocolor, Florence

Printed in Italy by Giunti Industrie Grafiche Spa, Prato
International Standard Book Number: 0-87226-616-8

99 00 01 02 03 15 14 13 12 11 10 9 8 7 6 5 4 3 2

Contents

Introduction

The dry, mountainous lands of Greece in the northeastern corner of the Mediterranean were the home of the Ancient Greeks, founders of the first great civilization in Europe. Ancient Greece occupied the same area as the earlier Minoan and Mycenaean civilizations and was influenced by them both. The many independent city-states that made up Classical Greece at its peak in the 5th century BC were brilliant centers of art, theater, scientific inquiry and political and philosophical debate. Today, 2,500 years later, their discoveries continue to influence ideas and events in Europe, America and many other parts of the world.

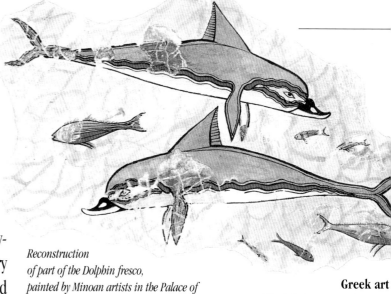

Reconstruction of part of the Dolphin fresco, painted by Minoan artists in the Palace of Knossos around 1600 BC. Only a few fragments of the original have survived.

These tiny terracotta statues were made in Boeotia around 2,500 years ago. They were children's toys.

Greek art

Highly skilled Greek craftspeople mastered a wide range of techniques. They made statues in bronze, marble and gold, produced and decorated pottery vases in all shapes and sizes, and made beautiful jewelry with gold and other precious metals and stones.

Plate with horses, dating to the 8th century BC.

The Greek world

This map shows the Greek world in around 850 BC as Greece emerged from the Dark Ages. Although the Greek influence would spread much further in the following centuries, this area remained the center stage of Greek language and culture until Alexander the Great splashed them across the Near East 500 years later.

Greek mythology

The Greeks had many wonderful myths about their gods, goddesses and heroes. The Ancient Romans adopted many of them and from them they were passed down to Renaissance times and then to the modern world.

Vase showing the twins Castor and Pollux, gods of shipwrecked sailors. The two were inseparable and when they died Zeus transformed them into the Gemini constellation.

GREECE

Locris

Megara
Corinth Athens

Sparta

Lesbos

Phokaia

Smyrna

Samos
Miletos

AEGEAN SEA

RHODES

CRETE

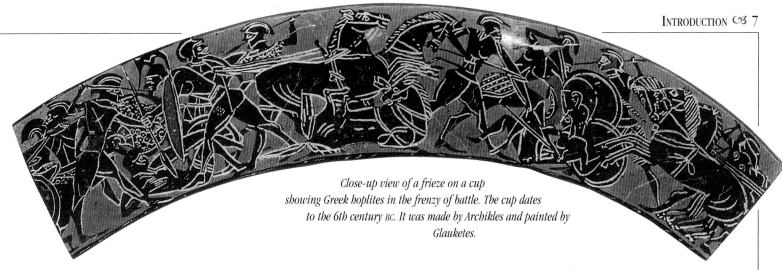

*Close-up view of a frieze on a cup
showing Greek hoplites in the frenzy of battle. The cup dates
to the 6th century BC. It was made by Archikles and painted by
Glauketes.*

Vase painting

Much of what we know about Greek rituals, religion and daily life comes from studying Greek vases which, from the 6th century onward, were decorated with scenes from mythology and life at the time. These vases were exported all over the Greek world, probably in exchange for basic food items, such as grain, olive oil and wine.

The François Vase

This large vase (it stands over 2 feet tall) was found in an Etruscan grave at Chiusi, Italy. Used as a wine-mixing bowl, it is one of the earliest Athenian vases to show mythological scenes. It has six friezes (rows of decoration) on each side with more than 200 figures acting out the scenes. The main frieze (1), which runs around the whole vase, shows a procession of gods and goddesses in honor of the newly weds Peleus and Thetis. The top frieze shows the Calydonian boar hunt (2) above the funeral games for Patroklos (3). Each handle shows a gorgon (4), Artemis with animals (5), and Ajax carrying the dead body of Achilles (6).

In 1900 the beautiful vase was shattered into 638 pieces by a museum attendant. It has been carefully restored.

The artists

The François Vase is signed by both the potter, Ergotimos, and the painter, Kleitias. Almost all the scenes and most of the objects are labelled with their names.

Minoans and Mycenaeans

Two major civilizations flourished on the Greek mainland and islands before the appearance of Classical Greece. The earliest, known as the Minoan civilization, after the legendary king Minos, dawned well over 2,000 years BC. It was based on the Mediterranean island of Crete and lasted until about 1450 BC, when it was destroyed by a combination of natural disaster and conquerors from the mainland. However, many of the great palace cities were soon rebuilt by the Mycenaeans, who also came from the mainland (and were probably the same people who had overrun the peace-loving Minoans). Mycenaean culture absorbed much from its forerunners, although it was never as lighthearted or beautiful. The wealthy Mycenaeans lived in heavily fortified hilltop towns. Their civilization died out during the 12th century BC, when it was either overrun by conquerors from the north or destroyed by civil war.

Gold face mask from the royal tombs at Mycenae.

Mycenae

Mycenae was one of the largest Mycenaean cities (and gives its name to the civilization). According to legend, it was the capital of Agamemnon, the famous king who sacked the city of Troy. Archaeologists have uncovered large areas of the walled city, including the graves of its wealthiest citizens. These contained masks, pottery, jewelry and other items of great beauty and value.

Minoan palaces

The Minoans built huge palaces on Crete, at Knossos (reconstruction shown left), Phaistos, Mallia and in several other locations. The Knossos palace, covering around 2 acres, was the largest of them all. Built on several levels, it was arranged around a rectangular courtyard where religious ceremonies were held. The upper floors were luxurious living quarters, while the rooms below served as workshops, warehouses and servants' rooms.

Skilled Minoan craftspeople produced beautiful objects in the palace workshops. They specialized in luxury items like the rhyton (vase) shown here. This was carved from a single piece of rock crystal. The handle is made from beads carved from rock crystal.

This bronze blade showing a dramatic Mycenaean lion hunt is decorated with inlays of gold, silver and black stone.

This gaming board, found at the palace of Knossos, Crete, was made by Minoan craftspeople. It is made of ivory, rock crystal, gold, silver and blue glass paste. Players probably rolled dice to play a game that was somewhere between modern backgammon and chess.

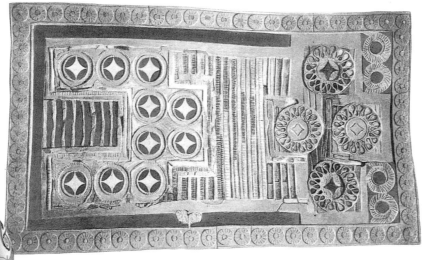

Mycenaean craftspeople produced beautiful pottery. Some pots had geometric designs while others showed animals or people. The distinctive style spread to islands in the eastern Mediterranean where it lingered even after the end of Mycenaean civilization.

Minoan sarcophagus showing a religious ceremony

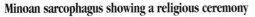

The sarcophagus (coffin), found at Haghia Triada on Crete and dating to around 1450 BC, is decorated with two frescoes of religious ceremonies (probably a funeral). On the left, it shows three women marching to the sound of the lyre (1). The woman on the far left (2), probably a priestess, is pouring liquid into a large vase (3). On the right, three men are carrying animals (4) and other offerings towards a figure, probably the person who died (5). The hairstyles (6) and clothing (7) of both the men and the women are typically Minoan in style.

A warlike people

The tombs of Mycenaean nobles have revealed an amazing array of bronze weaponry. Single tombs sometimes contained a dozen richly decorated swords and daggers along with a selection of knives, arrowheads and spearheads. The sturdy bronze suit of armor and helmet made from the tusks of 40 wild boars (above) would have belonged to a wealthy warrior.

The Archaic Period

The time between the end of Mycenaean civilization and the rise of Classical Greece in the 5th century BC is known as the Archaic period. Little is known of early Archaic times (12th–11th centuries BC) when the art of writing was lost and the population declined, and this period is called the "Dark Ages". Beginning in about 1000 BC, many people migrated from the Greek mainland to Asia Minor (now western Turkey) and the Aegean islands in search of better farmland. A northern people, known as the Dorians, settled in mainland Greece at this time. Then, during the 10th-century BC, conditions gradually improved as population increased and new towns and cities were founded. These small, independent communities were the forerunners of the unique city-states of late Archaic and Classical times.

Two examples of early Greek jewelry. The earring at the top, found in an 8th-century BC tomb at Athens, has intricate gold decorations. The earring on the left, in gold, was also found in a tomb in Athens. It dates to the mid-9th century BC.

This vase, dating to the 10th century BC, is one of the earliest of its kind. Greek vases at this time were decorated with abstract patterns rather than with human or animal figures. This pottery is known as "protogeometric."

The Dark Ages

Some light was shed on the Dark Ages in the 1980s when archaeologists discovered some very rich cemeteries at Lefkandi, on the island of Euboea. They found evidence of a bronze foundry and of trade with Cyprus, Egypt and Palestine dating to around 1000 bc. They also uncovered a large aisled building made of mudbrick resting on stone foundations. These finds suggest that, at least in one corner of Greece, the Dark Ages were not as backward as was once believed.

Statue of a bard (a traveling musician and storyteller), from the 8th century BC.

A terracotta centaur (half man, half horse) found at Lefkandi.

Population movements

As the Mycenaean world drew to a close there appear to have been quite large movements of people in various parts of the Aegean. Small waves of migration continued throughout the Dark Ages and the period was generally one of unsettled movement. At this time a people known as the Dorians appeared in mainland Greece and were said to have come from the north. Speakers of the "Dorian dialect" were greeted with hostility from other groups, such as the Ionians (whose most famous city was Athens), who they would not even allow them into their temples.

This painted clay model of a linen chest is decorated with five beehive-shaped granaries with trap doors. It is painted in the geometric style and was found in a 9th-century BC woman's cremation in Athens.

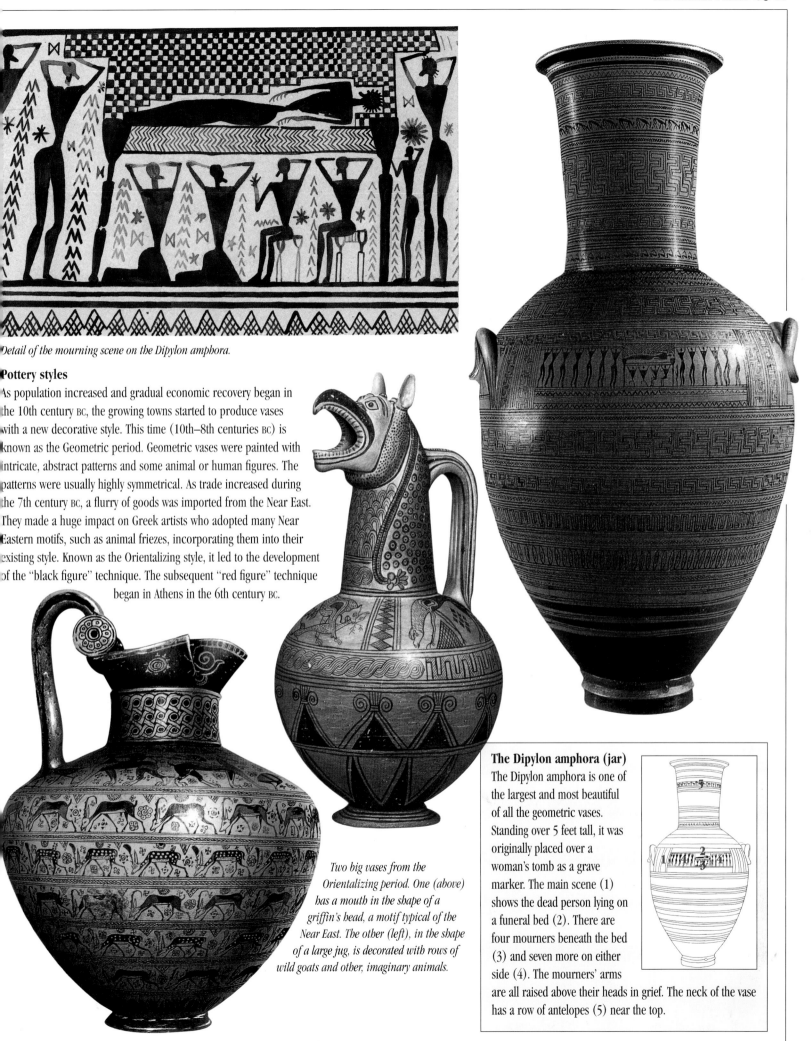

Detail of the mourning scene on the Dipylon amphora.

Pottery styles

As population increased and gradual economic recovery began in the 10th century BC, the growing towns started to produce vases with a new decorative style. This time (10th–8th centuries BC) is known as the Geometric period. Geometric vases were painted with intricate, abstract patterns and some animal or human figures. The patterns were usually highly symmetrical. As trade increased during the 7th century BC, a flurry of goods was imported from the Near East. They made a huge impact on Greek artists who adopted many Near Eastern motifs, such as animal friezes, incorporating them into their existing style. Known as the Orientalizing style, it led to the development of the "black figure" technique. The subsequent "red figure" technique began in Athens in the 6th century BC.

Two big vases from the Orientalizing period. One (above) has a mouth in the shape of a griffin's head, a motif typical of the Near East. The other (left), in the shape of a large jug, is decorated with rows of wild goats and other, imaginary animals.

The Dipylon amphora (jar)

The Dipylon amphora is one of the largest and most beautiful of all the geometric vases. Standing over 5 feet tall, it was originally placed over a woman's tomb as a grave marker. The main scene (1) shows the dead person lying on a funeral bed (2). There are four mourners beneath the bed (3) and seven more on either side (4). The mourners' arms are all raised above their heads in grief. The neck of the vase has a row of antelopes (5) near the top.

City-states

By about 750 BC almost all of Greece was divided into independent, self-governing communities known as city-states. A city-state, or *polis*, as the Greeks called them, was not like a modern city. The term refers to a community of people living in a town and the surrounding countryside who were bound together by a common legal and judicial system and also by a common spirit and shared mythology and religious beliefs. At first the city-states were dominated by aristocratic families and military leaders, but as time went on many of them developed more democratic forms of government. In some, male citizens were elected and they met together to discuss how the city-state should be run.

The several hundred city-states in Greece were quite similar in form. Each one was centered on a town, with protective walls(1) around it. There was usually an acropolis (2) on a hill in the center and an agora (3) nearby. Most were situated on a river (4) or near the sea (5) to facilitate transportation and trade.

Homer

Almost nothing is known about the life and background of the Greek poet Homer, author of the *Iliad* and the *Odyssey*. However, most scholars agree that he composed the poems (he may not have written them down; this may have been done after his death) during the 9th or 8th century BC. Homer's poems were very important to the ancient Greeks; they were the basis of Greek education and culture and well-educated people knew large parts of them by heart. They were valued as a symbol of Greek unity and a source of moral and practical guidance. The poems have been translated into many different languages and have continued to fascinate readers ever since.

A terracotta vase from Mykonos with an almost cartoon-like depiction of the Trojan horse episode from Homer's Iliad.

The Trojan horse

During the Orientalizing period Greek artists began to use themes from literature to decorate their vases. The Trojan horse scene above illustrates the well-known episode in the *Iliad* when the Greeks trick the Trojans into dragging a wooden horse filled with warriors inside the city walls. When the Trojans go to sleep that night the soldiers come out of the horse. Catching their enemies unawares, they are able to take the city and win the war. The scene is carved into the neck of a clay vase made in about 650 BC. It shows the horse (1) on wheels (2). Some of the Greeks are already outside the horse (3), while others are visible inside (4).

Both the Minoan and Mycenaean civilizations had written scripts. With the fall of the Mycenaeans, writing disappeared in Greece. This clay tablet is incised in the Mycenaean script, called Linear B. Scholars have decoded this script, which they recognize as an early form of Greek. The Minoans' Linear A script has not been deciphered. It is not a Greek language.

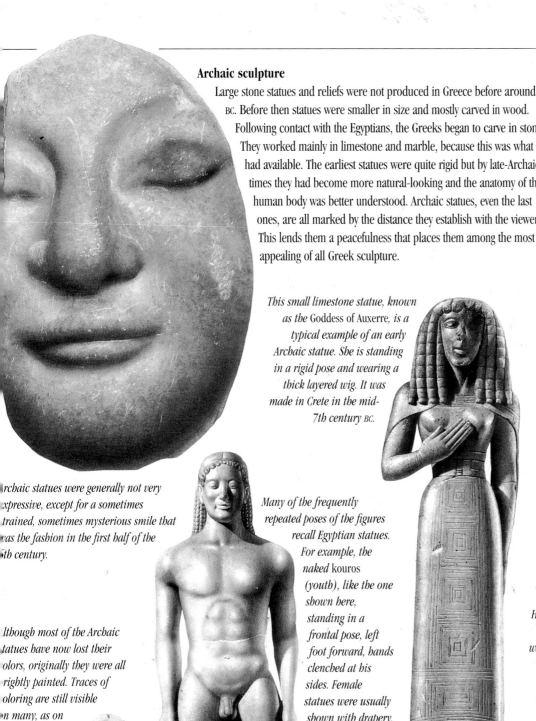

Archaic sculpture

Large stone statues and reliefs were not produced in Greece before around 680 BC. Before then statues were smaller in size and mostly carved in wood. Following contact with the Egyptians, the Greeks began to carve in stone. They worked mainly in limestone and marble, because this was what they had available. The earliest statues were quite rigid but by late-Archaic times they had become more natural-looking and the anatomy of the human body was better understood. Archaic statues, even the last ones, are all marked by the distance they establish with the viewer. This lends them a peacefulness that places them among the most appealing of all Greek sculpture.

This beautiful terracotta statue of the Greek goddess of fertility, Demeter, was made in a colony in Sicily (Italy). It dates to the late Archaic style and already shows a less rigid body posture.

This small limestone statue, known as the Goddess of Auxerre, *is a typical example of an early Archaic statue. She is standing in a rigid pose and wearing a thick layered wig. It was made in Crete in the mid-7th century BC.*

...rchaic statues were generally not very ...xpressive, except for a sometimes ...trained, sometimes mysterious smile that ...as the fashion in the first half of the ...th century.

Many of the frequently repeated poses of the figures recall Egyptian statues. For example, the naked kouros (youth), like the one shown here, standing in a frontal pose, left foot forward, hands clenched at his sides. Female statues were usually shown with drapery.

...lthough most of the Archaic ...tatues have now lost their ...olors, originally they were all ...rightly painted. Traces of ...oloring are still visible ...n many, as on ...his kore (girl) ...om Athens, ...culpted in ...round 510 BC.

Right: the head of a famous statue, known as the Rampin Horseman. Dating to the mid-6th century BC, it was placed in the Acropolis in Athens. The elaborate, tightly curled hairstyle is typical of statues in the late-Archaic style.

This reconstruction of a sculptor at work is based on a painting on a Greek vase.

Terracotta head of a warrior, made in Rhodes in the 6th century BC. Many of these tiny figures were produced in a range of shapes; they were used to hold perfume.

Religion and the Gods

Although the Greeks did not have a special word for religion, this doesn't mean that they had no gods or religious beliefs. On the contrary, they believed in many gods and goddesses and religion entered into most aspects of their daily lives. The 12 most important gods and goddesses, most of whom were Zeus's brothers, sisters or children, were believed to live in a sprawling palace on Mount Olympus. There was also another group of gods, gathered around the figure of Hades, god of the Underworld. These deities were believed to live inside the earth. Every village and town was dedicated to a god or goddess who was worshiped on a regular basis. Almost every group or gathering, including families, towns, sporting events, feast days, weddings, and funerals, was a religious event.

The oracle of Apollo at Delphi was the most importan[t] one for the Greeks. People came from all over th[e] ancient world to consult i[t].

The Olympian gods and goddesses

ZEUS: the chief god, and the god of justice; **HERA:** the jealous wife of Zeus she was worshiped throughout Greece; **APOLLO:** a powerful, widely worshiped god of religious law and the foundation o[f] cities. He was also the god of music, poetr[y] and dance; **ARTEMIS:** goddess of the hunt, nature, chastity and childbirth; **ATHENA:** goddess of war and crafts. She was the patron goddess of the city of Athens; **ARES:** a god of war and the spirit of battle; **APHRODITE:** goddess of love and beauty; **DEMETER:** goddess of grain and "Mother Earth"; **HEPHAESTUS:** blacksmith god of fire; **POSEIDON:** god of the sea, earthquakes and horses; **HERMES:** a fertility god. The messanger of the gods and the carrier of souls to the Underworld, also the god of shepherds; **HESTIA:** goddess of the home and family.

Right: Classical statue of beautiful Artemis, the goddess of wild animals and plants, the hunt, chastity and childbirth. She was the daughter of Zeus and Leto, and the twin sister of Apollo. Artemis was probably based on much earlier nature goddesses. Young Greek women danced in the woods in her honor. The goddess herself was believed to dance in the mountains, streams and wooded groves. She was the favorite goddess of country people.

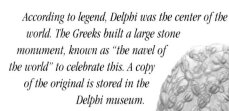

This 5th-century statue from Olympia shows the chief god Zeus carrying the boy Ganymede off to be his cupbearer on Mount Olympus.

This statue shows the goddess of love, Aphrodite, as the goat-footed satyr Pan tries to embrace her. The goddess has removed a sandal with which she is playfully threatening to strike him. A little Eros hovers above the goddess's shoulder and has seized hold of one of Pan's horns.

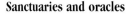

According to legend, Delphi was the center of the world. The Greeks built a large stone monument, known as "the navel of the world" to celebrate this. A copy of the original is stored in the Delphi museum.

Sanctuaries and oracles

Sanctuaries were important places of worship. They were dedicated to a god or goddess in gratitude for a fortunate event, such as winning a war, or surviving a famine or plague. Some sanctuaries had temples, gates and walls; others were simply marked out on the ground with a row of stones. There were hundreds of sanctuaries throughout Greece. Many sanctuaries also had oracles which people came to consult to find out about the future. Most important decisions, such as who[m] to marry, were only made after seeking the advice of an oracle. Even important questions of state, including whether to go to war, all required an oracular consultation.

This red figure vase (right) shows the gods Poseidon, Ares and Hermes fighting against four giants. It probably refers to the Battle of the Giants myth, according to which Mother Earth gave birth to the fearsome giants to punish Zeus. As soon as the giants were born they attacked Olympus, hurling lighted torches, boulders and flaming trees, forcing the Olympian gods to go war. To be killed, the giants had to be attacked at the same time by a god and a mortal. The battle went on for a very long time, and would never had ended had not the mortal hero Heracles joined in.

Mythology

Ancient Greek poets and playwrights left a rich store of myths and legends about their gods, goddesses and heroes. After Homer, authors such as Hesiod, Pindar, Aeschylus, Sophocles and Euripides, to name a few, recorded or composed works about Greek religion, creation stories, the activities of the gods, stories of human adventures and battle, and many others. These myths inspired Greek artists, and many of their statues and vase paintings show mythological episodes. The myths that were preserved have inspired poets and artists of European descent ever since.

Heracles leads Cerberus to Eurystheus

One of the best-known Greek legends tells of the 12 labors of Heracles. These were set for him by King Eurystheus. This vase painting shows the last labor, in which Heracles (1) brings Eurystheus the ferocious guard dog of Hades (the Underworld), called Cerberus (2). Cerberus had three heads and fearsome snakes rearing up off his muzzles and legs (3). With the help of the gods Athena and Hermes, Heracles was able to enter the Underworld and leave again with the dog (although he first had to wrestle with him). When Heracles arrived at the king's palace with Cerberus, Eurystheus was so frightened that he hid in a large jar (4). Afterward Heracles took the dog back to Hades.

This scene shows the return of the god Hephaestus to Olympus. Born lame, Hephaestus was expelled from Olympus as a youth, either by his mother Hera, or father, Zeus. Here he is shown with the clawed feet of an animal.

Priests and priestesses

As a general rule, male gods were tended by priests and female goddesses by priestesses. Their duties included supervising rituals, punishing people who broke sanctuary rules, and keeping the buildings in good order. Since most sanctuaries were only open a few days each year, priests and priestesses were not particularly busy or important.

This relief carving shows a priest and a priestess standing in front of an inscribed column with their arms raised in a typical gesture of prayer.

Processions were common in Greek festivals. Sometimes a small group, such as a family took part and sometimes, as in the Panathenaic festival held at Athens every year, the whole population paraded through the streets carrying gifts to the temple to offer the patron god or goddess of the city.

Feast days and holidays

Greek religion was not usually a somber affair, and the ancient calendar was punctuated with many feast days and festivals. The most important were annual festivals held to celebrate agricultural seasons or events, usually at sowing time, less often at harvest. Other feast days celebrated rites of passage, such as the registry of newly-married brides in their city or village quarter. Family ceremonies were held five days after the birth of a child, to welcome it into the household. There were also festivals to commemorate the dead, especially soldiers who had died in war.

Reconstruction of the procession during the Panathenaia (All-Athens festival). This festival was celebrated with special pomp once every fourth year when the Athenians brought a new woolen gown for the cult statue of Athena in the Parthenon.

A libation, the pouring of a liquid (wine, honey, olive oil, milk or water, or a mixture of these) onto an altar or fire was another way of honoring the gods or the dead. The man below is holding an olive branch as he performs the libation.

Sacrifices and offerings

Sacrifice was an important form of worship. Usually the victim was an animal, although other gifts, such as cakes or fruit, were also common. In a typical animal sacrifice, the thighbones of the sacrificial animal were wrapped in fat and burnt on the altar. The rest of the meat was cooked and eaten by the participants during a banquet that followed the sacrifice. Gifts to the gods were made on a regular basis and the gods were expected to receive a portion of the first harvest fruits, libations at drinking parties and a share of the catch from hunting trips.

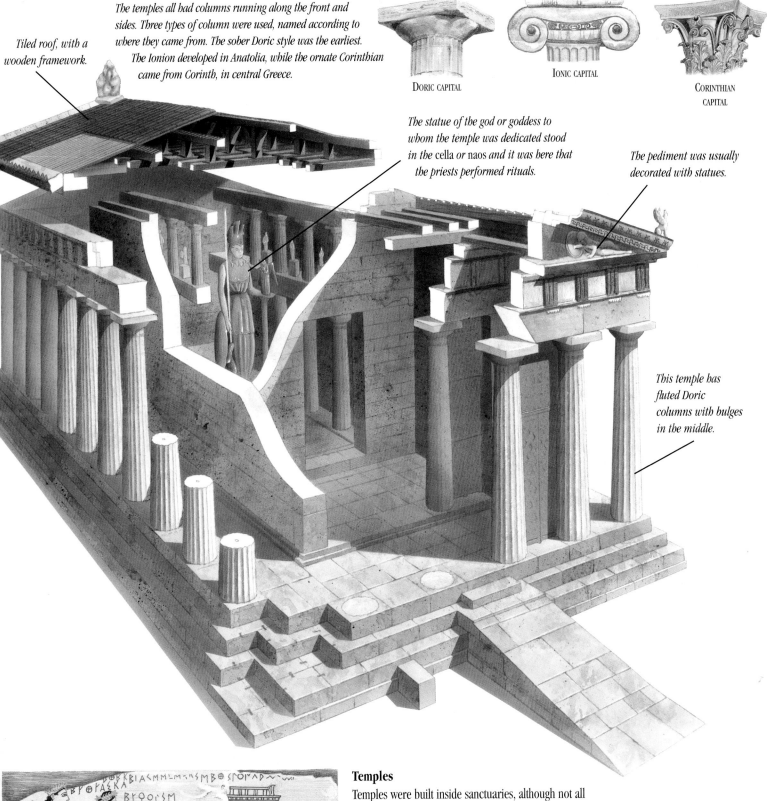

Tiled roof, with a wooden framework.

The temples all had columns running along the front and sides. Three types of column were used, named according to where they came from. The sober Doric style was the earliest. The Ionion developed in Anatolia, while the ornate Corinthian came from Corinth, in central Greece.

DORIC CAPITAL

IONIC CAPITAL

CORINTHIAN CAPITAL

The statue of the god or goddess to whom the temple was dedicated stood in the cella or naos and it was here that the priests performed rituals.

The pediment was usually decorated with statues.

This temple has fluted Doric columns with bulges in the middle.

This scene shows a lamb being led to the altar for sacrifice. It was found in the Pitsa cave at Corinth. Dating to over 2,500 years ago, it is very well preserved, even though it was painted on wood.

Temples

Temples were built inside sanctuaries, although not all sanctuaries had temples. The earliest temples, built during the 10th to 8th centuries BC, were simple wooden huts. These became more elaborate stone structures as the Greeks became richer and their architects more skilled. Temples always faced east–west in alignment with the sun. The altar was situated outside the temple, generally in front of it, presumably so that rituals could be performed in the open air where everyone could see them and take part.

Painted clay model of an early temple. Made in Argos in around 680 BC, it was dedicated to the goddess Hera.

Classical Athens

Athens was one of the largest and most powerful of the city-states. At its peak in the middle of the 5th century BC, it was a great center of learning, art and theater. It was also a pioneer in the areas of law and government. By this time all citizens had political rights and the People's Assembly and the popular courts were the main decision-makers. It was a democratic system, although it is important to remember that only men who had been born in Athens were considered "citizens." Women, foreigners and slaves, who made up the vast majority of the population, were excluded.

The statesman Solon was elected archon (chief magistrate) of Athens in 594 BC. He, and one of his successors Cleisthenes, passed laws that laid the framework for a more democratic society. Solon declared "The laws I passed were the same for rich and poor. My aim was to obtain justice for all."

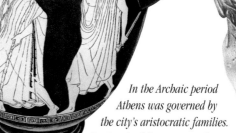

In the Archaic period Athens was governed by the city's aristocratic families. During the 6th century BC they were replaced by tyrannies. The vase painting below shows the assassination of the Hipparchus, tyrant of Athens, in 514 BC.

Pericles

Athens reached its zenith under the statesman and general Pericles (c. 495–429 BC). A highly educated man with broad political views, Pericles was responsible for rebuilding the city, which had been badly damaged during the sack of Athens by the Persians in 480 BC. He rebuilt the agora, improved the city's roads and enlarged the port of Piraeus. But his greatest undertaking was the construction of the Parthenon and the other buildings on the Acropolis. He also introduced far-reaching political reforms which gave more power to the poorer and less well-connected citizens.

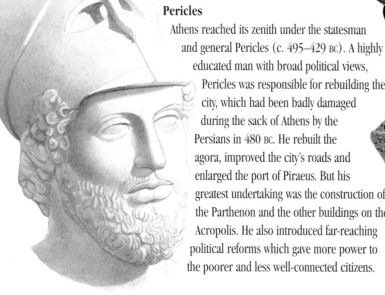

Head of Pericles, wearing a war helmet pulled up on his head.

The two wheels (below) are public ballots. They were used by voters to condemn or acquit someone on trial. Wheels with solid axles, like these ones, were used to acquit the defendant.

Pieces of pottery and ostraca, *like the ones shown below, were used to record the names of people who, by popular vote, were expelled from the city-state.*

Vase painting showing the citizens of Athens voting.

The Acropolis in Athens

The main temples and civic buildings of Athens were all on the Acropolis. This model shows the Acropolis in the 5th century BC when it was rebuilt after the Persian Wars. The Parthenon (1) was the main temple. On the left stood the Erechtheum (2), a beautiful Ionic temple dedicated to Athena. Next to it was the House of the Arrephoroi (3), where four young girls of noble birth lived. They wove a new *peplos* (gown) for Athena once every four years and performed rituals in her honor. A colossal bronze statue of Athena (4) in military dress stood behind the monumental entrance to the Acropolis, which was called the Propylaea (5). To the right was the Temple of Athena Nike (6), the goddess of victory. Behind it lay the Sanctuary of the bear goddess, Artemis Brauronia (7).

Gold statue of Athena, patron goddess of Athens, which stood in the Parthenon, the main temple on the Athenian Acropolis.

Statue of a woman grinding grain into flour. Bread was a staple food in the Greek diet and for many women grinding grain into flour and bread-making would have been daily chores. In large cities like Athens, bakeries were common and people could buy their bread ready-made.

Women were responsible for spinning wool into cloth and then weaving it into garments.

Household furniture was very simple, even in wealthy homes. Many pieces, such as couches, were used during the day for meals and at night for sleeping. This women (right) is placing some carefully folded linen away in a chest.

Women in Athens

Athenian women had few rights; they could not own property or gain protection from the law, nor could they take part in public life. Their lives revolved around their families. They cared for their husbands and children, ensuring that the household ran smoothly and that everyone had food, clothing and other daily necessities. In some ways poor women may have been better off than wealthy ones: at least they could leave the house to go shopping or to work without a chaperon.

Foreigners

Like all large cities, Athens attracted many foreigners. Some were freed slaves, but many others were merchants, traders and intellectuals. Even the wealthiest of them had no political rights. Pericles passed a law making citizenship even stricter: both parents had to be born in the city.

This scene from the inside of an Athenian cup of around 430 BC shows a reading lesson. The boy is reading from a folded wooden tablet, while the man reads from a scroll.

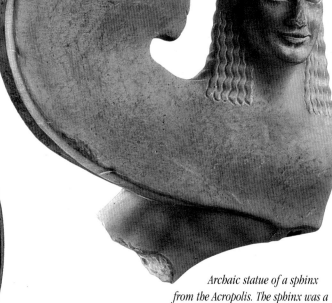

Archaic statue of a sphinx from the Acropolis. The sphinx was a typically eastern image that the Greeks adopted.

Education

Athenian citizens sent their sons to school at the age of seven. Although schooling had to be paid for, it was not very expensive and most boys would have had at least a few years education. There were three main subjects: literature, physical education and music. Literature included reading, writing, grammar and learning poetry, particularly Homer, by heart.

Craftwork

The central area of the city, around the marketplace, was crowded with workshops where craftspeople worked iron and bronze, made shoes, bags, pots, jewelry and other items. Most workshops were family-owned businesses with just a few people working in them. They sold their products one by one to the public who dropped by their premises, or bargained with merchants who took larger quantities to sell to clients in the local shops or for export.

Scene from a vase painting showing a cobbler's workshop. Sandals and shoes could be made to measure.

Clothing

Both men and women wore simple tunics, known as *chitons*, made from wool or linen. They were made from two squares of cloth sewn together down the sides. They were often held at the waist by a belt or girdle so that they fell in soft pleats. In winter they wore thick cloaks, called *himations*, over the top for extra warmth.

Right: two examples of some quite elaborate leather sandals. The Greeks wore a range of different kinds of shoe, including sandals, full shoes and pull-on or lace-up boots.

Scene in a blacksmith's workshop. The figure on the left is holding a piece of heated metal with tongs. The figure on the right is about to beat it into shape using an ax. A selection of tools are hanging on the wall behind.

The agora

The agora was an open space in the city center where citizens could meet. It was filled with stalls selling goods and surrounded by temples, shops, workshops and public buildings. Most men spent a part of each day in the agora talking to friends and discussing politics.

Three official measures, found in the agora in Athens.

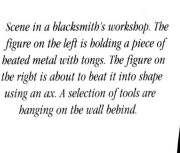

Many coins from Athens had images of owls on them. It was one of the symbols of the city.

Weights and measures

Official weights and measures were used for both dry and wet goods. Stamped with official marks, they came in varying sizes and shapes according to their use. Everyone used the same ones so that weights and measures were standardized. There were penalties for anyone who tried to give short measure.

Sparta

This clay head of a warrior was made near Sparta in about 700 BC.

The government and social organization of Sparta was unique among ancient Greek states. It was ruled by two lifetime kings, who had total power during wartime and only slightly less during times of peace, when they shared the task of ruling Sparta with a senate of 30 male citizens. In the 8th century BC Sparta developed a strong army and soon conquered its neighbors, whose citizens (known as "helots" by the Spartans) were kept almost in a state of slavery. Because the Spartans were outnumbered by their "subjects" by about seven to one, they were forced to maintain a powerful military and a rigid social order. All male citizens joined the army at five years of age and they stayed in it until they were thirty.

Spartan war helmet, probably of an aristocratic soldier. Spartan society was based on a military hierarchy of soldier castes, unified by a fierce discipline.

Spartan vase showing two wrestling scenes. In the larger scene, the man on the left has blood pouring from his nose, but the fight continues.

The origins of Sparta

According to legend, Sparta was founded in the 9th century BC, although there are few records from this very early period. During the 8th century BC the Spartans conquered neighboring Messenia, a land that was "good to plow and good to hoe" (in the words of the Spartan poet Tyrtaeus). This was a turning point for Sparta, which from then on needed a strong army to subdue its large subject population. State land was allotted to citizens and the conquered helots worked on it, giving a half of what they produced to their rulers.

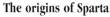

This Athenian vase painting shows Helen, wife of the Spartan king, Menelaus, with Priam, king of Troy. According to Greek legend, the Trojan war broke out when Priam's son Paris, kidnapped Helen and took her back to his homeland.

The Peloponnesian War (431–404 BC)

Sparta and Athens were the most powerful city-states in ancient Greece. They each commanded alliances of other states and between them they controlled almost the entire Greek world. When war broke out between the two in 431 BC, it was brutal and devastating. The Athenians, who had many overseas colonies, were richer and commanded a powerful navy. The Spartans, however, could count on their well-trained army. The war, which involved costly battles (many as far away as southern Italy), dragged on until 405 BC when the Athenian fleet was finally destroyed by the Spartans. Athens itself surrendered the following year.

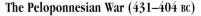

• Athens

• Sparta

Aegean Sea

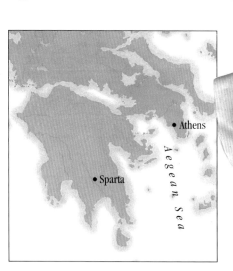

Bust of the Spartan military commander Pausanias, who led the combined Greek army to victory against the Persians in the Persian wars. He was later accused of treason and then suspected of plotting an uprising against Sparta. He sought refuge in a temple which the Spartans walled up while he was still inside. He starved to death in the temple.

The vase of Vix

This large bronze vase was found in the grave of a Celtic princess just south of Paris, France. However, it was clearly made by a Greek artisan working in Sparta in the late 6th century BC. The detail reproduced above is taken from the neck of the vase which shows seven ferocious Spartan warriors and seven war chariots. The foot soldier (1) is nude except for his elaborate helmet (2) and large shield (3). Four sturdy horses (4) are pulling the lightweight war chariot carrying the second warrior (5). The artist has skillfully captured all the ominous power that Spartan warriors were widely believed to inspire.

Below: the vase of Vix.

Spartan women

Greek women did not enjoy very much personal freedom. In wealthy households the women's quarters were separate from the main part of the house. Respectable women were not allowed to leave the house without a male companion. Girls generally were not sent to school, nor did they take part in physical training in most parts of Greece. Only in Sparta do records show that girls were allowed to train as athletes and take part in some sporting events. Spartan women may have enjoyed more freedom and power in other areas of life as well.

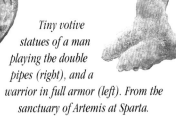

Tiny votive statues of a man playing the double pipes (right), and a warrior in full armor (left). From the sanctuary of Artemis at Sparta.

Colonies and Trade

Between the 8th and 6th centuries BC the Greek city-states founded colonies in many parts of the Mediterranean and around the shores of the Black Sea. Founding a colony was a formal undertaking; a leader was chosen, magistrates were appointed who would parcel out the land in the new colony, and an oracle was consulted to choose the best time and place. Surprisingly, the new colonies were independent of their founding cities from the outset. The settlers themselves never returned to their homelands, although some contact was maintained through trade. The colonists spread the Greek language and ways everywhere they settled. The Greek influence was spread even farther afield through the extensive trade routes they developed.

The Greeks founded several colonies on the coast of Thrace (modern Bulgaria), the most important of which was Constantinople (modern Istanbul). The silver rhyton (drinking horn) left, made in Thrace during the 4th century BC, shows a mixture of Greek and Thracian elements.

This 4th-century BC Phoenician glass vase was found on the Mediterranean island of Sardinia, the southern part of which was a Phoenician colony.

Reconstruction of a vase-maker's house at Locri, in southern Italy. Pottery amphorae (jars), vases, jugs and containers of every sort were in high demand for transporting and storing oil, wine and water.

The Phoenicians

The ancient land of Phoenicia lay in the Levant, where Lebanon is today. The Phoenicians were excellent sea-traders and colonizers. By the time the Greeks began to colonize the Mediterranean, the Phoenicians already controlled the coasts of North Africa and much of Spain. Although rivals, the two powers traded and also exchanged ideas. For example, the Greek alphabet is based on the much earlier Phoenician one.

Jars going off
to be sold

Well

Finished jars

Kiln

Cla[y] statue of [a] youth on horseback from a temple a[t] Locri, souther[n] Italy. The horse i[s] resting on [a] sphinx[.]

Magna Grecia

There were so many Greek colonies in southern Italy and Sicily that the area became known as *Magna Grecia* (Greater Greece). The region's closeness to Greece, its good farmland and many natural harbors, made it an obvious choice for settlement. Colonies were limited to the south, because of the powerful Etruscan civilization that contolled central Italy at the time (although there was frequent contact between the two). The Romans absorbed much of what they knew of Greek culture from the southern colonies.

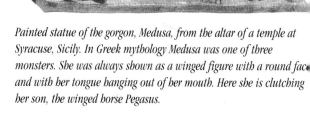

Painted statue of the gorgon, Medusa, from the altar of a temple at Syracuse, Sicily. In Greek mythology Medusa was one of three monsters. She was always shown as a winged figure with a round face and with her tongue hanging out of her mouth. Here she is clutching her son, the winged horse Pegasus.

Colonies and trade

The map shows the main colonies and trade routes around the Mediterranean and Black seas from about 800–500 BC. The Greeks are mainly concentrated in southern Italy and France and in the Black Sea area. The Phoenicians control the Levant and much of North Africa and southern Spain.

CORNWALL

Phoenicia
Phoenician colonies
Greek homelands
Greek colonies
Etruscan states
Tin route to Cornwell
Phoenician trade routes
Greek trade routes

SPAIN

ETRURIA

Black Sea

ANATOLIA

SYRIA

MAGNA GRECIA

GREECE

RHODES

CRETE

LEVANT

NORTH AFRICA

Mediterranean Sea

EGYPT

Bronze griffin from a wine bowl. The griffin is a typically Eastern motif. It was made in a Greek city in Asia Minor in around 650 BC.

Illustration of the Nereid Monument as reconstructed in the British Museum. Built in the form of a small Ionic temple (originally at Lycia in Asia Minor), it shows a mixture of Greek and Persian attributes.

The Black Sea colonies

During the 8th century Greek colonizing efforts were concentrated mainly on Italy. During the 7th and 6th centuries they concentrated more on Thrace and the Black Sea regions. The Greek colonies in these areas traded Greek-made luxury goods with the people of the steppes for wheat to feed the cities in the Greek homeland. Colonies in North Africa (Cyrenaica and Egypt), were also founded at about this time.

Statue of the Greek goddess Aphrodite, made by the Bactrian people in central Asia. The Greek influence spread far beyond the colonies themselves.

The Near East

By 900 BC the coastal areas of Anatolia and the island of Rhodes were part of Greece itself. One of the first colonies in the Near East was founded at Al Mina, in Syria. The Persians and the Egyptians only allowed the Greeks to set up small trading colonies in the areas they controlled. The colony at Al Mina, for example, stood at the head of an overland route to Mesopotamia.

Below: bronze statue of an African slave. There were thousands of slaves in ancient Greece and almost every household owned at least one. Wealthy families could own as many as fifty.

This vase painting shows a wild boar being caught. Hunting was a popular sport among wealthy Greeks. Wild boars, deer and hares were common catches. However, hunting was always more of a sport than a main source of meat. Fishing, on the other hand, was widely practised and fish were an important source of protein in the Greek diet.

What was traded

Generally speaking, the cities of mainland Greece imported basic necessities, such as cereals, olive oil, wine and salt-fish, from their colonies and from neighboring countries. They paid for these goods with luxury items, including pottery, jewelry and other craftwork. Other commonly traded goods included timber, minerals, slaves, marble and glass.

Skillful Greek craftspeople made beautiful pottery vases, many of which were painted with mythological scenes. They also made intricate jewelry and art objects.

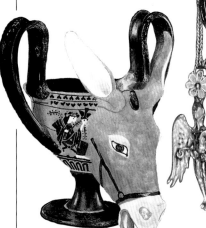

Vase showing farmers harvesting the olives by shaking them out of the trees using long sticks.

Farming

The hilly Greek countryside, combined with its hot, dry summers and cold winters, does not make Greece an ideal place for farming. Only about 20 percent of the land was suitable for growing vegetables, wheat and other cereals. The lower slopes of the hills were used to grow olives and grapes. Even so, agriculture formed the basis of the Greek economy. Most farms were small, family-run operations.

As the populations of the cities of mainland Greece increased, so did the need for basic foodstuffs. Records from Athens show that the city was dependent upon the arrival of wheat in the city port of Piraeus. The local government passed laws forcing merchants to land their goods there.

Painted plate from Cyrene

This painting shows King Arkesilas II (1), of the Greek colony of Cyrene (in modern Libya), scepter in hand (2), as he oversees a bustling trading scene. Some of his servants (2) are carrying sacks (probably of dried herbs, for which the colony was famous) to be weighed, while others appear to be filling up sacks and taking note of weights (3). The merchandise was probably being prepared for export to the Greek mainland. The scales are held in place by a stork (4) and other animals. The leopard cub (5), lizard (6) and monkey (7), all typically African animals, remind us where the scene is taking place.

Money

Metal coins began to be used to pay for goods during the 7th century BC in Anatolia (modern Turkey). Their use spread quickly throughout the Greek world. Each city-state minted its own coins, decorated with local designs, such as the heads of rulers or local products.

Trade and commerce

Small merchants operated from the craft workshops near the central marketplace. As trade developed, larger merchants began to operate in the ports, where they offered ships for hire and generally controlled imports and exports. Many became very rich, not just from trading but also from loaning money to other traders (often at very high interest rates).

Scene from a vase painting showing a sleek pirate galley speeding after a merchant ship. Piracy was a problem and some city-states sent their merchant fleets out in groups protected by the navy.

War

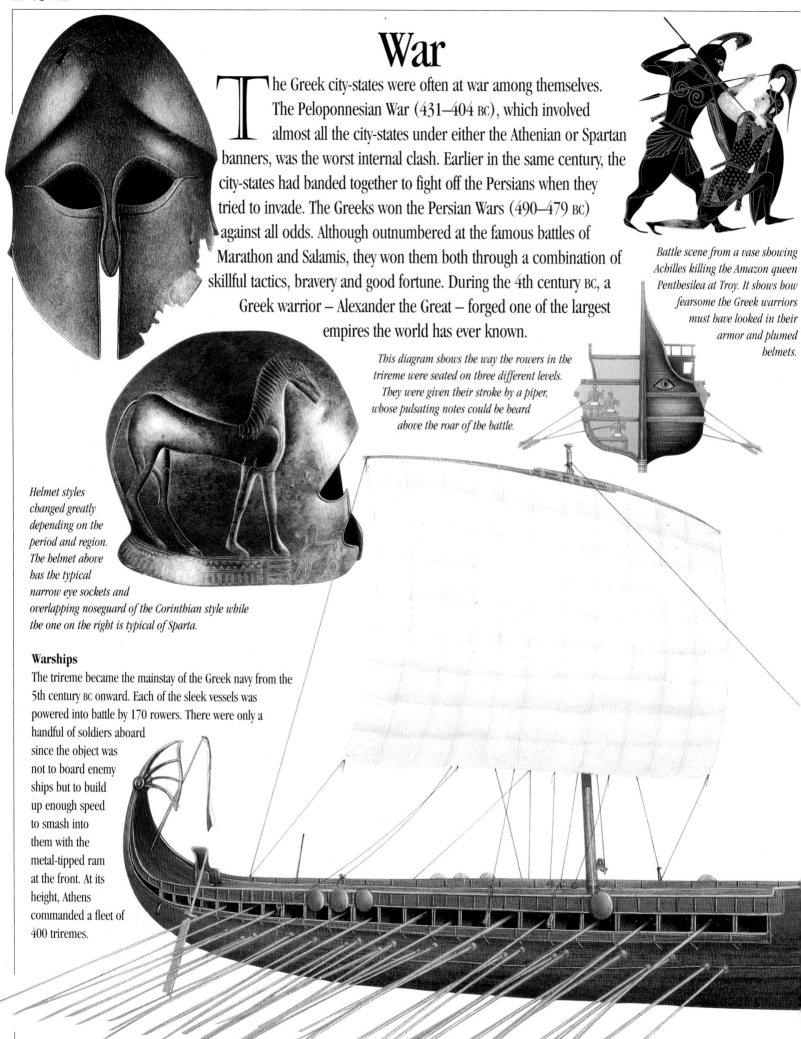

The Greek city-states were often at war among themselves. The Peloponnesian War (431–404 BC), which involved almost all the city-states under either the Athenian or Spartan banners, was the worst internal clash. Earlier in the same century, the city-states had banded together to fight off the Persians when they tried to invade. The Greeks won the Persian Wars (490–479 BC) against all odds. Although outnumbered at the famous battles of Marathon and Salamis, they won them both through a combination of skillful tactics, bravery and good fortune. During the 4th century BC, a Greek warrior – Alexander the Great – forged one of the largest empires the world has ever known.

Battle scene from a vase showing Achilles killing the Amazon queen Penthesilea at Troy. It shows how fearsome the Greek warriors must have looked in their armor and plumed helmets.

This diagram shows the way the rowers in the trireme were seated on three different levels. They were given their stroke by a piper, whose pulsating notes could be heard above the roar of the battle.

Helmet styles changed greatly depending on the period and region. The helmet above has the typical narrow eye sockets and overlapping noseguard of the Corinthian style while the one on the right is typical of Sparta.

Warships

The trireme became the mainstay of the Greek navy from the 5th century BC onward. Each of the sleek vessels was powered into battle by 170 rowers. There were only a handful of soldiers aboard since the object was not to board enemy ships but to build up enough speed to smash into them with the metal-tipped ram at the front. At its height, Athens commanded a fleet of 400 triremes.

Greek foot soldiers in battle

This painting on a 7th-century BC vase made at Corinth, shows hoplites (foot soldiers) engaged in battle. They are all carrying long lances (1) and brightly painted shields (2), and wearing protective breastplate armor (3), plumed helmets (4) and greaves to protect their knees and shins (5). To the left (6) a piper is playing flute music while they fight.

Reconstruction of a Greek warrior in full battle gear.

The diagram below shows a phalanx of Greek soldiers ready to attack the enemy. This was a typical formation, with row upon row of armored warriors pouring forth. When the soldier in the front line got hit and fell to the ground his place was immediately taken by the one behind. This meant that the ranks were never broken.

Weapons and tactics

Soldiers in the Classical period were usually armed with long lances, but they often had throwing spears, arrows, slings and swords too. Up until the 5th century BC, most soldiers were citizens of the city-state they fought for. As such, they were expected to supply their own armor and weapons and richer men had to bring their own horses. Paid armies of professional soldiers developed during the Peloponnesian War in the 5th century.

Entertainment

Wealthy, city-dwelling Greeks had plenty of leisure time and there was a wide variety of activities they could take part in, either as participants or spectators. Public entertainment included theater, poetry readings accompanied by music, dancing and sporting events. At home men enjoyed evening banquets and drinking parties, where they discussed philosophy and politics (and probably gossiped as well). Dancing and music was provided by actors and musicians. Respectable women, who lived fairly secluded lives, also had their parties and dinners, although we know rather less about them. Children had toys and games and pets, much as they do today.

Scene at a wealthy drinking party. The male guests are lounging on beds where they are being entertained by women. Two little tables in the foreground are littered with wine goblets.

Symposiums and drinking parties

Greek men liked to dine in the company of friends in the evenings and they held dinner parties, which were called symposiums. The guests arrived at dusk and began with dinner. Depending on how wealthy their host was, they would eat a meal of fish, oysters and other seafood, bread, cheese, poultry, meat, some vegetables, and olives. The guests' hands were then washed and fruit was brought in for dessert. Wine was served throughout the meal. Afterwards the tables were cleared and the drinking party began. The guests talked, played games, recited poetry and were entertained by professional musicians and dancers.

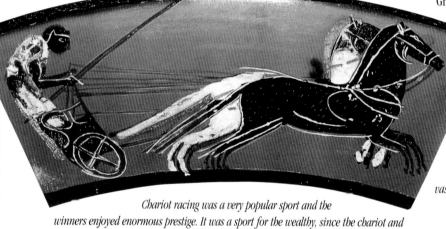

Chariot racing was a very popular sport and the winners enjoyed enormous prestige. It was a sport for the wealthy, since the chariot and horses were expensive. Sometimes professional charioteers were used.

This vase, painted by the famous vase painter, Exekias, shows the Greek heroes Ajax and Achilles playing drafts.

Sports

Sports were perhaps the most highly regarded form of entertainment and the Greeks took them seriously. Young men were expected to train every day to develop their fitness and physical attractiveness. A well-proportioned body was considered the outward sign of a developed mind. The most common sports were running, long jump, wrestling, discus, javelin throwing, boxing and horse racing. In most places women were not permitted to take part in sporting events. Sparta seems to have been the exception to this and records show women athletes competing there.

Athletes competed in the nude. These men are running what must be a sprint, since their pumping hands and legs suggest speed rather than the endurance required for marathons.

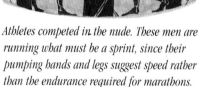

Statue of a boxer resting, from the 1st century BC. His hands, wrapped with "gloves," and the open wounds on his face, show just how violent this sport could be.

Vase painting with a theater scene

This 4th-century BC vase shows a scene from a comedy. In Greek theater there were normally only three actors on the stage at once (all men, even if they were dressed as women). In this case, a circus acrobat (1), standing on his hands, and a comic actor wearing a very ugly mask (2), are facing toward the seated figure of an actor representing Dionysos (3). Above, to the left and right of the acrobat, two female theatrical masks (4) are framed in the windows. All actors wore masks the whole time they were on stage.

Toys and games

Children played with spinning tops, knucklebones (like the girl shown here, left), wooden and clay toys, rattles, and dolls. They also had board games, such as snakes and ladders and drafts. Many children also kept pets, including cats, dogs, hens, ducks, monkeys and tortoises.

These painted clay figures were children's toys.

A teacher instructing two youths how to play the lyre.

Theater

The Greeks enjoyed going to the theater, probably because the plays they saw were so very good. Many of the works that have survived from Classical times are still considered some of the greatest ever written and they are still performed today. Plays were put on in steep-sided, open-air theaters. Sometimes, as in the great spring festival in Athens – the City Dionysia – spectators sat from dawn until dusk for four consecutive days watching the latest plays by the best dramatists.

Music

Music was the constant companion of most activities in ancient Greece, not only the obvious ones like dancing or at banquets and feast days, but also during war, athletic competitions and everyday work situations, such as baking bread. Boys were taught to play instruments and to sing at school. Learning music and song was thought to have a civilizing effect on *"the boys minds, to make them less wild, and better in tune for effective discourse and action..."*

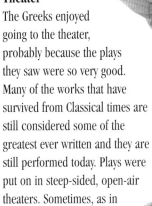

Sculpted head of the first great Athenian playwright Aeschylus. His most famous works include Agamemnon, The Furies *and* Prometheus Bound.

The Alexander mosaic

This huge Roman mosaic (it measures almost 20 x 10 feet) is a copy of an earlier Greek painting. It celebrates Alexander the Great's victory over the Persian king, Darius III. Both leaders are clearly visible: Alexander on the left (1), mounted on horseback and without a helmet, and Darius on the right (2), on a retreating war chariot and wearing a helmet. Battle rages all around them. In the center foreground a horse has fallen (3) and his rider is picking himself up as Alexander bears down on him, stabbing him with his long lance (4). Behind Darius, to the left and right, long lances point skyward. (5).

The famous Three Graces *group was found in Siena, Italy, during the early Renaissance. Dating to the Hellenistic period, the statue (and, more generally, the theme) was copied many times by Renaissance artists.*

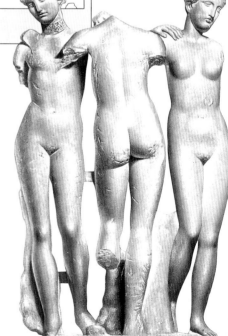

This 4th-century lion mosaic comes the royal palace of Pella, home to the kings of Macedonia. Lion hunting, a sport imported from the Near East, was a favorite pastime for Macedonian kings and also a common motif for artists.

The Hellenistic Period

The Hellenistic period (336–31 BC) covers the 300 years or so between the reign of Alexander the Great and the rise of the first Roman Emperor, Augustus. This was the time in which Greek culture, although weakened at home, spread across western Asia, as far east as northern India. Alexander the Great conquered a vast empire which split into three main kingdoms on his death in 323 BC. These kingdoms were: the Macedonian (Alexander's homeland, north of Greece), the Seleucid (from Anatolia to Persia), and the Ptolemaic (in Egypt). Although there were frequent wars between the three, the Greek language and culture united the region. It was a highly creative time, at least until about 160 BC, when the growing power of Rome began to cast its shadow over the Greek world.

Marble head of a youthful Alexander, attributed to the Greek sculptor Leochares.

Alexander the Great

Alexander III of Macedonia was born in Pella in 356 BC. He came to throne just 20 years later when his father was murdered. Alexander quickly consolidated his power at home and then set off on a journey of conquest that took him east as far as India. His empire, which stretched for over 20,000 miles, remained under Greek control until the Romans took over 300 years later.

This dynamic bronze statue of Alexander the Great on a rearing horse (probably his favorite, Bucephalus), was made in Roman times. Of all the portraits, it best catches the spirit of Alexander's life.

Aristotle

One of the two greatest Greek philosphers, Aristotle, (384–322 BC) grew up at the royal court of Macedonia, where his father was a doctor. When his father died, he was sent to Athens to study under the other great philosopher, Plato. In 342 BC Aristotle returned to the Macedonian court where he was tutor to the young Alexander for three years. On returning to Athens he founded an important school. Aristotle's writings deal with every branch of human knowledge. They have influenced both Western and Muslim thought greatly over the centuries.

Coin with the head of Ptolemy I of Egypt (364–283 BC).

The Venus de Milo, showing the goddess Aphrodite, is one of the most famous works of Greek art. It was sculpted during the 2nd century BC.

Hellenist art and science

The Hellenist age was an inventive time, both in the fields of art and science. Works of art became more expressive and some of the best-known pieces of Greek art, including the *Venus de Milo* and the *Laocoon* group, date to this time. The great mathematician Euclid, best-known for his treaty on geometry, lived during the Hellenistic period. Advances were also made in technology.

Alexandria

Alexander the Great founded the Egyptian city of Alexandria in 332 BC. It became the capital of his new Egyptian dominion and the base for his navy. When Alexander died Ptolemy took power and founded a dynasty in his name. Within a century of its founding Alexandria became the greatest city in the world and a center of Greek learning. The largest Greek library in antiquity, containing almost 500,000 book rolls, was kept in the city. The library was destroyed during a civil war in the 3rd century AD.

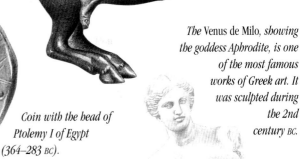

Reconstruction of the lighthouse of Alexandria, which stood in the ancient quarter of Pharos. It was considered one of the Seven Wonders of World.

The Greek Influence

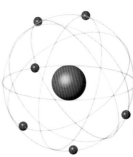

Greek culture and ideas have probably influenced subsequent societies, particularly in Europe and America, more than those of any other ancient civilization. The Romans, who conquered what remained of Alexander the Great's empire, were the first of many to borrow from Greek institutions and ideas. During the Renaissance, in 14th to 16th-century Europe, there was a huge revival of interest in Greek and Roman art, literature and thought. Greek influence has continued right up to the present and it is difficult to think of an area of modern life which has not been touched by the Greeks; from the Greek alphabet, which lies at the basis of most written languages in the West, to political concepts (such as democracy), and modern science and medicine, not to mention the fields of sport (including the Olympic Games), art and philosophy.

The English poet, Lord Byron, was one of many artists of the 19th-century Romantic era who were inspired by ancient Greece. Byron was so impressed by the Greek heritage that he joined the fight to liberate it from the Turks. While in Greece he caught a fever and died at just 36 years of age.

Diagram of an atom. In the 5th century BC Greek thinkers proposed that all things in nature were made up of basic particles, which they called "atoms." As in many other areas of scientific thought, modern science has shown that, substantially, the Greeks were right.